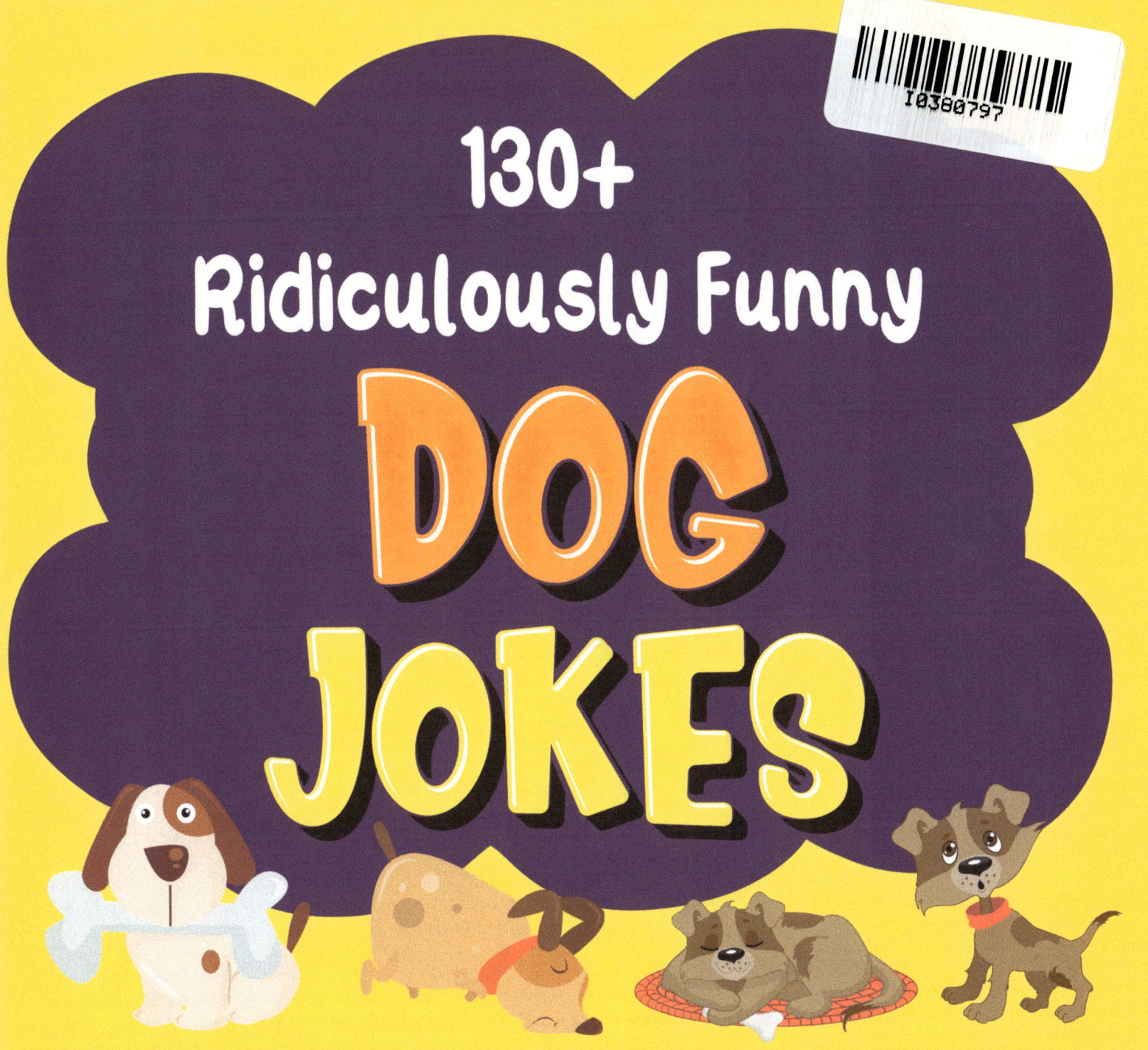

A teacher asks her class: "Let's say I gave you two dogs, two more dogs, and then another two dogs; how many would you have?" Wilma answers: "Seven."

Teacher: "No, Wilma, let me repeat the question... If I gave you 2 dogs, 2 more dogs and then another 2, how many would you have in total?" Wilma: "7."

Teacher, getting frustrated now: "Pff, OK...Let's try this another way. If I gave you two bananas, two more bananas, and then another two, how many bananas would you have?"

Wilma: "Six."

Teacher: "Exactly! Now, if I gave you two dogs, two more, and another two; how many would you have?" Wilma: "Seven!"

Teacher: "Wilma, where on earth do you get seven from?!" Wilma: "Because I already have a dog at home!"

Q: What did the cat say, when he saw the dog had trashed his pillow?
A: You got to be kitten me.

Q: Why don't blind people like to skydive?
A: Because it really scares their guide dog!

Q: What is a dog's favorite city?
A: New Yorkie!

One Saturday morning, a wife says to her husband: "Our dog is so smart. He brings in the daily newspapers every single morning!" Her husband replies: "Yes, he's a great dog, but lots of dogs can do that." "Yes, but we've never subscribed to any," the wife responded.

Q: Where does a Rottweiler sit in the cinema?
A: Anywhere it wants to!

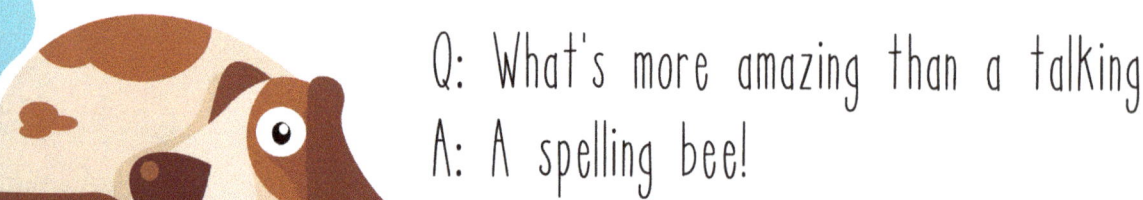

Q: What's more amazing than a talking dog?
A: A spelling bee!

A labrador walks into a job center. "Wow, a talking labrador," says the clerk. "With your talent, we will definitely be able to find you a job in the circus." "The circus?" says the polar bear, disappointed: "Why would a circus want to hire a lawyer?"

Q: What do you call a large dog that meditates?
A: Aware wolf!

Q: What do you get when you cross a dog and a calculator?
A: A friend you can count on!

Q: What kind of dog chases anything red?
A: A Bulldog!

Q: What kind of dog did Dracula have?
A: A bloodhound.

Q: Why do dogs make terrible dance partners?
A: They've got two left feet!

Q: Why did the poor dog chase his tail?
A: He was trying to make both ends meet.

Q: Where does a Rottweiller sit in the cinema?
A: Anywhere it wants to!!

Q: How do you know your dog is stupid?
A: When it chases parked cars!

One day, a police officer was sitting in his car with his K9 partner in the back seat. A little girl approached the car and asked the officer: "Is that a dog in the back seat?" The officer replied: "Yep, it sure is!" To which the girl responded: "Wow, what did he do?"

Q: What's a dog's favorite kind of pizza?
A: Pupperoni.

Q: What happened when the dog went to the flea circus?
A: He stole the show!

Q: What sort of clothes does a pet dog wear?
A: A petticoat!

Two moms discuss how to get their sons to wake up in the morning, to get them to school on time. "How do you get your sleepy-head son up in the morning?", the first mom asked. The other mom replied: "I just put the cat on the bed." "Huh, how does that help?" The other mom: "The dog's already there..."

Q: Why does the dog bring toilet paper to the party?
A: Because he is a party pooper!

While walking her dog, a girl is stopped by an office. He asks her for her dog's license. To which she responds, "My dog is only 4, he doesn't drive!"

Q: Why was the cat scared of the tree?
A: Because of its bark.

Q: What dog wears contact lenses?
A: A cock-eyed spaniel!

Two chihuahuas are sitting on opposite sides of a river. One chihuahua yells to the other: "How do I get to the other side of the river?" To which the other chihuahua replies: "You ARE on the other side!"

Q: What do you get when you cross a race dog with a bumble bee?
A: A Greyhound Buzz!

A dog sits in a bar, sipping a whiskey. A customer walks up to him and says, "Wow, it's not often that I see a dog drinking bourbon here!" To which the dog replies: "Yeah, but that's hardly a surprise at these prices."

Q: What looks like a dog, eats dog food, lives in a doghouse, and is very, very dangerous?
A: A dog with a machine gun.

Q: Why didn't the dog speak to his foot?
A: Because it's not polite to talk back to your paw!

Knock, knock!
Who's there?
Ron.
Ron who?
Ron a little faster, will you? There's a Pitbull after us!

Did you hear about the dog who had puppies on the sidewalk? She was ticketed for littering!

Q: Why did the dog cross the road twice?
A: He was trying to fetch a boomerang.

Q: What is a dog's favorite food?
A: Anything on your plate!

One day, a man visited his friend. When he walked into the living room, he found his friend playing checkers with a German Shepherd. Astonished, he watched the game for a couple of minutes. "I can't believe my eyes!" he exclaimed. "That is the smartest dog I have ever seen." To which his friend replied: "Mwoah, he's not that smart. I've beaten him three games out of five."

A man drives deep into the woods to get rid of his dog. He lets him out at an abandoned place. After 30 minutes, his wife calls him: "The dog is back..." The man growls: "Oh man...Ehm, can you put him on, please? I got lost and need directions..."

A traveler sits down in a restaurant to get lunch. All of a sudden, a bear walks in, buys a chocolate ice cream and leaves. The traveler is astounded: "Wow, that's so weird!" The restaurant manager: "Yeah, I agree, up until today he always ordered strawberry ice cream."

Q: What do you call a dog with a surround system?
A: A sub-woofer.

Q: What do you call a dog magician?
A: A labracadabrador!

Q: What do you call a frozen dog?
A: A pupsicle.

A dog went to the post office to send a telegram. He took out a blank form and wrote: "Woof. Woof. Woof. Woof. Woof. Woof. Woof. Woof. Woof." When he was done, he gave it to the clerk. The clerk looked at the paper and said to the dog: "There are only 9 words here. We have a special offer: You could send another 'Woof' for the same price." To which the dog replied: "Sorry, but that wouldn't make any sense at all!"

Q: What do you get if you cross a dog and a lion?
A: Well you won't be getting any mail, that's for sure.

Q: What do you call a dog with a fever?
A: A hot dog.

Q: What did the dog say when he sat on sandpaper?
A: Ruff!

While mending fences out on the range, a very religious cowboy lost his favorite Bible. He was devastated! Three weeks later, however, a dog walked up to him, carrying that same Bible in its mouth. The cowboy was astonished, he couldn't believe it! He took the precious book out of the dog's mouth, thanked him, went on his knees and exclaimed: "It's a miracle!". To which the dog replied: "Not really. Your name is written inside the cover."

Q: What do you call a dog who designs buildings?
A: A bark-itect!

Q: What's a dog's favorite dessert?
A: Pupcakes!

Q: What did the hungry Dalmatian say after his meal?
A: "That hit the spots!"

Did you hear about the Pomeranian who invented the knock knock joke? She won the no-bell prize!

Knock, knock!
Who's there?

Ken.
Ken who?
Ken you walk the dog for me?

Knock, knock!
Who's there?
Doughnut.
Doughnut who?
Doughnut pull my dog's tail, or he'll bite you!

Q: Why do dogs run in circles?
A: Because it's hard to run in squares!

At a royal dinner party, a beagle farts. The king turns to him and says: "How dare you fart in front of me!" The beagle replies: "I'm terribly sorry, your highness, I didn't realize it was your turn!"

Two friends were walking their dogs on a Friday afternoon. One had a Pitbull and the other had a Chihuahua. Then the guy with the Pitbull said: "I'm thirsty, let's get a drink in that bar over there." To which his friend replied: "I don't think they will allow our dogs in there." The one with the Pitbull responded: "Just follow my lead, trust me."

The guy with the Pitbull put on a pair of sunglasses and walked into the bar. The bouncer at the door said: "I'm sorry man, but there are no pets allowed inside." The man with the Pitbull replied: "But this is my guide dog, I am helpless without him!". Bouncer: "A Pitbull?". The man: "Yeah, they're using Pitbulls now too, they're amazing!".

Bouncer: "Okay, come on in." The other man then also put on his sunglasses. He thought: a Chihuahua is even more unbelievable, but it's worth a try. So, the bouncer stopped him, and said: "Sorry no pets allowed." To which the man replied: "This is my guide dog, I am lost without him."
Bouncer: "Really, a Chihuahua?". To which the man replied: "Whhaaat? They gave me a fricking Chihuahua?!"

Q: What do your dog and a cellphone have in common?
A: They both have collar I.D.

Q: What do you get when you cross a herding dog and a daisy?
A: A Collie-flower!

Q: Which dog breed will laugh at all of your jokes?
A: A Chi-ha-ha!

Q: What did the dog say to the flea?
A: Stop bugging me!

Q: In what month do dogs bark the least?
A: February, it's the shortest month!

Q: What do you do if your dog eats your pen?
A: Use a pencil instead!

    Q: What time is it when ten dogs chase a cat?
    A: Ten After One.

Q: Why was the dog such a good storyteller?
A: He knew how to paws for dramatic effect...

My dog's been having a bad day. When I came home, I asked him: "How's life?" All he said was: "RUFF..."

Q: Why did the dog sleep under the car?
A: Because he wanted to wake up oily.

Q: Which breed of dog is the quietest?
A: A hush puppy!

Q: What is the fastest dog in the world?
A: A Labraghini.

Q: What do you get if you cross a dog with a frog?
A: A dog that can lick you from the other side of the road!

Q: What kind of dog likes taking a bath?
A: A shampoodle!

I went to the zoo today, there was only one animal. It was a Shih Tzu...

John: "I have a dog that doesn't have a nose". Bill: "And how does he smell?" John: "Awful!"

Q: What do you call a dog with a Rolex?
A: A watchdog.

One day, a pug walks in a store and asks the shop owner if he sells cranberries. The shop owner says, "No, we only sell strawberries." The next day, the pug returns and asks for cranberries again. Again, the shop owner says he doesn't.

When the pug returns the very next day, the shop owner says: "No, stupid pug, we don't sell cranberries! If you come back tomorrow with that same question again, I swear I will nail your paws to the floor!" The shop owner can't believe his eyes when the pug walks into his store the next day. This time, the pug asks, "Do you have any nails?" The shop owner replies, "No, we don't." "Okay, good," the pug responds, "Do you sell cranberries?"

Two convicts are about to break out of prison. The first one jumps off a wall into a trash container. The guard, alarmed by the noise, shouts "Who's there?". The criminal replies, "Woof Woof!" The guard is relieved, "Ah I see, it's just a dog." Then, the second convict jumps, also making some noise. The guard now gets suspicious and asks, "Hello, who is there?" To which the second convict replies, "Nobody, it's just the dog again!"

Q: What is a dog's favorite instrument?
A: A trombone.

Q: What did the cat say to the dog?
A: Check meow-t!

Q: What happens when a dog chases a cat into a geyser?
A: It starts raining cats and dogs.

Q: What do you get if you cross a dog and a cheetah?
A: A dog that chases cars – and catches them!

Q: What do you get when you try to cross a Pitbull with a computer?
A: A lot of bites.

Q: What happens when you cross a rooster, a Cocker Spaniel and a Poodle?
A: A Cockerpoodledoo!

A man takes his poodle to the vet, because he is cross-eyed. The vet says: "Let's have a look" and picks up the poodle to examine his eyes. After looking at his eyes for a while, the vet says: "I'm going to have to put him down." "Wait, what?" the man replies, "Just because he is cross-eyed?" Vet: "No, because he is really heavy!"

Q: How do you stop a dog from barking in your front yard?
A: Put it in your back yard.

Q: How did the little Scottish dog react when he met the Loch Ness Monster?
A: He was Terrier-fied!

Q: What do dogs eat for breakfast?
A: Pooched eggs.

Q: What's a dog's favorite sound?
A: The dinner bell.

Q: Where do dogs go after their tails fall off?
A: The re-tail store.

Q: Why do Dog Vampires believe everything you tell them?
A: Because they're suckers!

Q: What do you call a black Eskimo dog?
A: A dusky husky!

Q: Why can't dogs work the TV remote when watching Netflix?
A: Because they always hit the Paws button!

Q: What did the waiter say to the dog when he brought out her food?
A: Bone appétit!

Q: Why shouldn't you bring your farty dog to an Apple store?
A: Because they don't have Windows!

Q: What happens when you name your dog after Kim Kardashian?
A: You give a dog a bad name.

Q: What do scientist dogs do with bones?
A: Barium!

Q: How do fleas travel from place to place?
A: By itch-hiking!

Q: What is it called when a cat wins a dog show?
A: A CAT-HAS-TROPHY!

Q: What do you get when you cross a Doberman with a Saint Bernard's?
A: A dog that bites you and then goes to fetch help.

On a dark night, a burglar breaks into a house. As he reaches to steal some valuables, he hears a voice say: "Jesus is watching you." The burglar jumps up and hides behind the curtain. He peaks around the corner but doesn't see anybody. So, he goes back to the valuables and continues putting them in his bag. "Jesus is watching you," the voice says once more. This time, the burglar looks harder and he sees a parrot.

"Who are you?" he asks. The parrot replies, "Constantine." "Wait, what? Who on earth would call a parrot Constantine?" the burglar responds, relieved. "I don't know," says Constantine, "I guess the same kind of people that would call a Rottweiler Jesus."

Q: Why do dogs like conjunctions?
A: They just love buts.

Q: What do you get if you cross a rottweiler and a hyena?
A: I don't know but I suggest you join in if it laughs!

Q: What do you do when you find a 250 pound dog sleeping on your bed?
A: Quietly go sleep on the sofa...

Q: What is the difference between a dog and a mailbox?
A: So you don't know? OK, in that case I think I'll mail that letter myself, thank you.

Q: What kind of dog eats with their ears?
A: They all do! Who removes their ears before dinner?

Q: What dog can jump higher than a tree?
A: Any dog can jump higher than a tree. Trees can't jump!

Q: What do you call a cold dog?
A: A Chili Dog.

Q: Why did the snowman name his dog "Frost"?
A: Because he bites!

Q: What's a dog's favorite study subject?
A: Barkeology.

Q: What happens when it rains cats and dogs?
A: You can step in a poodle!

Q: What do you call a dog with no legs?
A: It doesn't matter: he's not going to come anyway.

Q: How are a dog and a marine biologist alike?
A: One wags a tail and the other tags a whale.

Q: Why don't dogs bark at their feet?
A: Because it's not polite to talk back to your Paw.

Q: What do you call a sleeping Rottweiler?
A: Anything you like, just very quietly.

John: "When I get older I am getting a dog." Mom: "Awesome, what's his name going to be?" John: "Naked." Mom: What, why? John: "So when my friend's come over, I can tell them I am walking naked down the street!"

Q: Why did the dog stay in the shade?
A: Because he did not want to turn into a hot dog.

Q: Who is the dog's favorite comedian?
A: Growlcho Marx!

Q: What's a dog's favorite flower?
A: Any flower in then garden!

Q: What do you do if a dog chews your dictionary?
A: Take the words right out of his mouth!

Q: What do you get if you cross a sheepdog with a jelly?
A: The collie wobbles!

A three-legged dog walks into a bar. He says: "I'm looking for the man who shot my paw!"

Q: What do you get if you cross a Beatle and an Australian dog?
A: Dingo Starr!

One day, a man walks into a bar one day and asks, "Does anyone here own that bull terrier outside?" "Yeah, I do!" a trucker says. "What about it?" "Well, I think my chihuahua just killed him..." "What are you talkin' about?!" the trucker says, in disbelief. "How could your tiny dog kill my bull terrier?" "Well, it seems he got stuck in your dog's throat!"

Q: What happened when the golden retriever went to the flea circus?
A: She stole the show!

Q: What do you call a dog that can use the toilet?
A: A 'poo-dle'.

Q: What did the dog say to the tree?
A: Bark!

Q: What happened to the dog that swallowed a firefly?
A: It barked with de-light!

Q: What happened when the golden retriever went to the flea circus?
A: She stole the show!

Q: When is a mom flea happy?
A: When her whole family has gone to the dogs.

Walking past a veterinary clinic, a man noticed a young girl and her dog waiting outside. 'Are you here to see Dr Johnson?' he asked. 'Yes,' the girl said. 'I'm having my dog put in neutral.'

John: "When I get older I am getting a dog." Mom: "Awesome, what's his name going to be?" John: "Naked." Mom: What, why? John: "So when my friend's come over, I can tell them I am walking naked downtown!"

Q: How can you tell the difference between a labrador and a marine biologist?
A: The one wags a tale, the other tags a whale!

Q: What did the hungry Dalmatian say when he had some kibble?
A: That hit the spot!

Q: Why do dogs bury bones in the ground?
A: Because you can't bury them in trees!

Q: What did the cowboy say when the bear ate his German shepherd?
A: "Well, doggone!"

Q: What do you get if you take a really big dog out for a walk?
A: A Great Dane out!

www.ingramcontent.com/pod-product-compliance
Lightning Source LLC
Chambersburg PA
CBHW051401110526
44592CB00023B/2912